The Essential Guide to Digital Marketing

Naveen Sharma

Published by Naveen Sharma, 2024.

Table of Contents

Chapter 1: Introduction to Digital Marketing 1

Chapter 2: The Foundations of Digital Marketing 4

Chapter 3: Search Engine Optimization (SEO) 8

Chapter 4: Content Marketing 13

Chapter 5: Social Media Marketing 18

Chapter 6: Email Marketing 24

Chapter 7: Pay-Per-Click Advertising (PPC) 29

Chapter 8: The Future of Digital Marketing 35

Chapter 9: The Digital Marketing Revolution: A Modern Fairytale 40

FAQ: Digital Marketing 43

References of Successful People Who Achieved Success Through Digital Marketing 49

Conclusion 52

This book is dedicated to the dreamers, the innovators, and the relentless entrepreneurs who see possibility where others see limitation. To the small business owners building their brands from the ground up and to the marketers who constantly push the boundaries of creativity and strategy.

To my family and friends for their unwavering support and encouragement throughout this journey. Your belief in me has been my driving force.

And finally, to all the readers who are ready to embrace the digital world, I dedicate this guide to you. May it empower you to take bold steps, explore new opportunities, and achieve your greatest potential.

Chapter 1: Introduction to Digital Marketing

1.1 Understanding Digital Marketing

Digital marketing is a term that you've probably heard a lot, but what does it really mean? In simple terms, digital marketing is the way businesses use the Internet and other digital channels to reach their customers. Unlike traditional marketing, which might use things like newspapers, TV commercials, or billboards, digital marketing focuses on using online platforms like websites, social media, and email.

Imagine you have a small store that sells handmade jewelry. In the past, you might have relied on word-of-mouth, flyers, or maybe a local newspaper ad to attract customers. But now, with digital marketing, you can reach people far beyond your local area. You can show your jewelry to people all over the world by using social media or a website. Digital marketing gives you tools to connect with your audience in ways that were never possible before.

1.2 Why does Digital Marketing matter?

So, why is digital marketing so important? The answer is simple: because that's where your customers are. Today, almost everyone uses the internet. They search for products, read reviews, watch videos, and interact with brands online. If your business isn't using digital marketing, you're missing out on a huge opportunity to reach and engage with your customers.

Let's take an example. Suppose you're running a coffee shop. You could rely on people walking by and noticing your shop, but what if you could also reach people who are looking for a cozy place to have coffee in your area? By using digital marketing, like creating a Google My Business profile or running a local ad on Facebook, you can attract more customers who are specifically looking for what you offer.

Digital marketing is not just about selling products or services; it's about building relationships with your customers. It allows you to interact with them, understand their needs, and offer solutions that make their lives easier. This connection can turn one-time buyers into loyal customers who come back again and again.

1.3 The Purpose of This Book

The world of digital marketing can seem overwhelming, especially if you're new to it. There are so many tools, strategies, and platforms that it can be hard to know where to start. That's why this book is here to guide you through the basics and beyond.

In this book, you'll learn everything you need to know to get started with digital marketing. We'll break down each topic into simple, easy-to-understand language, so you can apply what you learn to your own business. Whether you're a small business owner, an aspiring marketer, or someone who simply wants to understand how digital marketing works, this book will give you the knowledge and confidence to succeed.

By the end of this book, you'll have a clear understanding of how digital marketing can help your business grow. You'll learn how to create a strong online presence, connect with your audience, and use different digital marketing strategies to reach your goals.

So, let's dive in and explore the exciting world of digital marketing together!

Chapter 2: The Foundations of Digital Marketing

2.1 Building a Strong Online Presence

In today's digital world, having a strong online presence is the foundation of any successful digital marketing strategy. But what does it mean to have an online presence? Simply put, it means that your business is easily found and recognized online. This usually starts with having a website, but it also includes being active on social media, having online reviews, and appearing in search results.

Why is this important? Think about the last time you searched for a product or service. Where did you look first? Most likely, you went online. If a business doesn't show up when someone searches for what they offer, they miss out on potential customers. That's why building a strong online presence is the first step in digital marketing.

Creating a Website: Your website is like your digital storefront. It's often the first place potential customers will go to learn about your business. A good website should be easy to navigate, provide clear information about what you offer, and make it simple for visitors to contact you or make a purchase.

If you don't have a website yet, don't worry! You don't need to be a tech expert to get started. There are many user-friendly tools and services that can help you create a professional-looking website without needing to know how to code.

Social Media Profiles: In addition to a website, it's important to have profiles on social media platforms where your customers are active. Social media allows you to engage directly with your audience, share updates, and promote your products or services. It's also a great way to build your brand's personality and connect with customers on a more personal level.

Start by creating profiles on popular platforms like Facebook, Instagram, or LinkedIn, depending on where your target audience spends their time. Keep your profiles up-to-date, post regularly, and interact with your followers to keep them engaged.

2.2 Understanding Your Audience

Knowing who your customers are and what they want is a crucial part of digital marketing. When you understand your audience, you can tailor your marketing efforts to meet their needs, which leads to better results.

Identifying Your Target Audience: Your target audience is the group of people who are most likely to be interested in your products or services. To identify your target audience, start by thinking about the characteristics of your ideal customer. This could include factors like age, gender, location, income level, interests, and behaviors.

For example, if you own a fitness studio, your target audience might be young adults who are interested in health and wellness.

Understanding these details will help you create marketing messages that resonate with your audience.

Why Understanding Your Audience Matters: When you know who your audience is, you can create content and ads that speak directly to them. This increases the chances that they will engage with your brand and eventually become customers.

One way to learn more about your audience is by gathering data. You can do this through surveys, social media insights, and website analytics. These tools can provide valuable information about who your audience is, what they're interested in, and how they interact with your brand.

2.3 Crafting a Digital Marketing Strategy

Once you have a strong online presence and understand your audience, it's time to create a digital marketing strategy. A strategy is like a roadmap that guides your marketing efforts and helps you achieve your business goals.

Setting Clear Goals: The first step in crafting a digital marketing strategy is setting clear goals. What do you want to achieve with your digital marketing? Your goals might include increasing website traffic, generating leads, boosting sales, or building brand awareness. Make sure your goals are specific, measurable, and achievable.

For example, instead of saying "I want more customers," a specific goal would be "I want to increase website traffic by 20%

in the next three months." Having clear goals will help you focus your efforts and measure your success.

Choosing the Right Channels: Next, decide which digital marketing channels you will use to reach your audience. These channels could include your website, social media, email marketing, search engine optimization (SEO), and pay-per-click (PPC) advertising. The channels you choose should align with your audience's preferences and your business goals.

Creating a Content Plan: Content is at the heart of digital marketing. Whether it's blog posts, social media updates, videos, or emails, the content you create should provide value to your audience. A content plan outlines what kind of content you will create, how often you will post, and where you will share it.

For instance, if your goal is to drive traffic to your website, you might create a blog that provides helpful tips related to your industry. You can then share these blog posts on social media and in your email newsletters to reach a wider audience.

Tracking and Adjusting Your Strategy: Finally, it's important to track the results of your digital marketing efforts. Use analytics tools to monitor your performance and see if you're meeting your goals. If something isn't working, don't be afraid to adjust your strategy. Digital marketing is constantly evolving, and being flexible will help you stay ahead.

Chapter 3: Search Engine Optimization (SEO)

3.1 What is SEO?

Search Engine Optimization, or SEO, is a term that might sound complicated, but it's actually quite simple once you break it down. SEO is all about making your website easier to find on search engines like Google. When someone searches for something online, search engines show a list of websites that are most relevant to that search. SEO helps your website show up higher in these search results, which means more people are likely to visit your site.

Think of it like this: If you own a bakery, and someone in your area searches for "best bakery near me," you want your bakery's website to appear at the top of the search results. The higher your website ranks, the more likely it is that people will click on it. SEO is the process of optimizing your website so that it ranks higher and gets more visitors.

Why is SEO Important? SEO is important because it helps you get noticed by people who are looking for what you offer. Unlike ads that you pay for, SEO brings in visitors naturally, or "organically." This means you don't have to pay each time someone clicks on your website. Plus, people tend to trust organic search results more than paid ads, so SEO can help build credibility for your business.

3.2 On-Page SEO

On-page SEO refers to the things you can do on your website to help it rank higher in search results. This includes optimizing your website's content, structure, and code. Here are some simple ways to improve your on-page SEO:

Using Keywords: Keywords are the words and phrases that people type into search engines when they're looking for something. For example, if you run a pet store, keywords like "buy dog food" or "pet supplies" might be important for your website. By including these keywords in your website's content, search engines can better understand what your site is about and show it to people searching for those terms.

However, it's important not to overdo it. Keywords should fit naturally into your content. If you stuff too many keywords into your text, it can make your content hard to read and might even hurt your rankings.

Creating Quality Content: Content is king when it comes to SEO. Search engines love websites that provide valuable, relevant information to users. This could be blog posts, articles, product descriptions, or even videos. The more useful your content is, the more likely it is to be shared and linked to by others, which can boost your rankings.

Make sure your content is clear, informative, and easy to read. Break up long paragraphs, use headings to organize your text, and include images or videos to make your content more engaging.

Optimizing Titles and Descriptions: The title of each page on your website is important for SEO. It should be descriptive and include your main keyword. For example, instead of just "About Us," you might use "About Our Pet Store | Your Source for Quality Pet Supplies."

Meta descriptions are short summaries that appear below the title in search results. While they don't directly affect your rankings, they can influence whether people click on your link. A good meta description should be clear, include your keyword, and encourage people to visit your site.

3.3 Off-Page SEO

Off-page SEO refers to actions taken outside of your website that can help improve its ranking. This mainly involves getting other websites to link back to your site, which is known as building backlinks. Backlinks are like votes of confidence from other websites, showing search engines that your site is trustworthy and valuable.

Building Backlinks: One of the best ways to build backlinks is by creating high-quality content that others want to link to. For example, if you write a helpful blog post about caring for pets, other websites might link to it as a resource. You can also reach out to other websites and ask them to link to your content, especially if it complements what they offer.

Another way to get backlinks is by guest posting on other blogs or websites. By writing an article for another site, you can include a link back to your own website. This not only helps with SEO but also exposes your business to a new audience.

Social Media and SEO: While social media links don't directly impact your rankings, being active on social platforms can still help with SEO. When your content is shared on social media, it increases its visibility and the chances that other websites will link to it. Plus, social media profiles often show up in search results, so maintaining an active presence can help improve your overall online visibility.

3.4 Local SEO

If your business serves a local area, local SEO is especially important. Local SEO helps your business appear in searches made by people in your area. This is particularly useful for businesses like restaurants, salons, or stores that rely on local customers.

Optimizing for Local Search: To optimize your website for local search, make sure to include your business's name, address, and phone number on your website. This information should be consistent across all your online listings, such as on Google My Business, Yelp, and social media profiles.

Google My Business: One of the most effective tools for local SEO is Google My Business. This free tool allows you to create a profile that shows up in Google search results and on Google Maps. Your profile can include your business's location, hours of operation, contact information, and even customer reviews. By keeping this profile updated, you can improve your chances of appearing in local search results.

Chapter 4: Content Marketing

4.1 What is Content Marketing?

Content marketing is a powerful tool in digital marketing that focuses on creating and sharing valuable content to attract and engage an audience. Instead of directly promoting a product or service, content marketing provides useful information that helps your audience solve problems, learn something new, or entertain them. The goal is to build trust and establish your brand as an authority in your industry, which can lead to more customers over time.

Imagine you own a gardening store. Instead of just telling people to buy your products, you could create content like blog posts, videos, or how-to guides that teach people how to garden. By providing helpful tips and advice, you attract people who are interested in gardening. They learn to trust your brand, and when they're ready to buy gardening supplies, they're more likely to choose your store.

Why Content Marketing Matters: Content marketing is important because it helps you connect with your audience on a deeper level. It's not just about selling; it's about building relationships. When you provide valuable content, you show that you care about your customers' needs, which can lead to long-term loyalty.

Content marketing also helps improve your SEO efforts. Search engines love fresh, relevant content, and by regularly updating your website with new content, you can improve your chances of ranking higher in search results. This means more people will find your website when searching for information related to your industry.

4.2 Creating Valuable Content

Creating valuable content is the heart of content marketing. The key is to focus on your audience's needs and interests, rather than just promoting your products or services. Here are some tips to help you create content that resonates with your audience:

Understand Your Audience: Before you start creating content, it's important to know who you're creating it for. What are their interests? What challenges do they face? What kind of information are they looking for? Understanding your audience will help you create content that speaks directly to them.

Choose the Right Format: Content can come in many different formats, including blog posts, videos, podcasts, infographics, and more. The format you choose should depend on what your audience prefers and the message you want to convey. For example, if you're explaining a complex process, a video tutorial might be more effective than a written article.

Focus on Quality Over Quantity: It's better to create a few pieces of high-quality content than to churn out a lot of low-quality content. Your content should be well-researched, informative, and engaging. It should also be easy to read and understand. Break up long text with headings, bullet points, and images to make it more digestible.

Provide Solutions: Your content should help your audience solve a problem or answer a question. For example, if you run a health and wellness blog, you might write an article about how to reduce stress naturally. By providing practical advice and actionable tips, you show your audience that you're there to help them, not just sell to them.

Tell a Story: People love stories, and storytelling can make your content more engaging and memorable. Share stories about your brand, your customers, or your industry. For example, if you own a bakery, you might write a blog post about how you started your business and the challenges you overcame. This personal touch can help your audience connect with your brand on an emotional level.

4.3 Distributing Your Content

Creating great content is just the first step; you also need to make sure it reaches your audience. Content distribution is the process of sharing your content across various channels to get it in front of the right people. Here are some ways to distribute your content effectively:

Social Media: Social media platforms like Facebook, Instagram, Twitter, and LinkedIn are excellent channels for distributing your content. Each platform has its own unique audience, so tailor your content to fit the platform you're using. For example,

Instagram is great for sharing visually appealing content, while LinkedIn is better for professional and industry-related content.

Email Marketing: Email marketing is a powerful way to distribute content directly to your audience. By sending regular newsletters or updates, you can keep your subscribers informed about new content, promotions, and events. Make sure your emails are well-designed and include clear calls to action that encourage readers to visit your website or engage with your content.

Your Website: Your website should be the central hub for all your content. Regularly update your blog or news section with new articles, videos, or other types of content. Make sure your content is easy to find and navigate, with clear categories and tags.

Content Syndication: Content syndication involves sharing your content on other websites or platforms to reach a broader audience. This can include guest blogging, republishing your content on platforms like Medium, or sharing it with industry-related websites. By syndicating your content, you can increase its reach and attract new followers to your brand.

Collaborations and Partnerships: Partnering with other businesses or influencers in your industry can help you reach new audiences. For example, you might collaborate on a blog post, co-host a webinar, or participate in a podcast. These partnerships can help you tap into your partner's audience and build your credibility.

SEO and Organic Search: Optimize your content for search engines to ensure it reaches people who are searching for information related to your industry. Use relevant keywords, create compelling titles, and make sure your content is easy to read and navigate. Over time, this will help your content rank higher in search results, attracting more organic traffic to your website.

Chapter 5: Social Media Marketing

5.1 The Power of Social Media

Social media has become a central part of our daily lives. People use platforms like Facebook, Instagram, Twitter, LinkedIn, and TikTok to connect with friends and family, share updates, and discover new things. For businesses, this presents a unique opportunity to reach and engage with customers in a way that wasn't possible before.

Social media marketing involves using these platforms to promote your products or services, build your brand, and connect with your audience. It's not just about posting updates; it's about creating meaningful interactions that resonate with your followers and encourage them to engage with your brand.

Why Social Media Matters: Social media is important because it allows you to reach a large audience quickly and efficiently. It's a place where you can showcase your brand's personality, share your story, and build relationships with your customers. Unlike traditional marketing, social media allows for two-way communication, meaning you can interact with your audience in real-time.

For example, if you run a clothing store, social media can be a great way to showcase new arrivals, share fashion tips, or even run contests and promotions. The key is to be authentic and engage with your audience in a way that feels natural and relatable.

5.2 Choosing the Right Platforms

Not all social media platforms are created equal, and each one has its own strengths and audience. It's important to choose the right platforms for your business based on where your target audience spends their time and what kind of content you want to share.

Facebook: Facebook is one of the largest social media platforms, with billions of users worldwide. It's a great platform for businesses that want to reach a broad audience and share a variety of content, including text posts, images, videos, and links. Facebook also offers powerful advertising tools that allow you to target specific demographics and interests.

Instagram: Instagram is a visually-focused platform that's popular with younger audiences. It's ideal for businesses that want to showcase products, share behind-the-scenes content, and engage with their audience through images and videos. Instagram Stories and Reels are particularly effective for sharing short, engaging content that captures attention quickly.

Twitter: Twitter is known for its fast-paced, real-time content. It's a great platform for sharing news, updates, and engaging in conversations with your audience. Twitter is also a valuable tool for customer service, as it allows businesses to respond quickly to customer inquiries and feedback.

LinkedIn: LinkedIn is a professional networking platform that's best suited for B2B (business-to-business) marketing. It's a place where you can share industry news, insights, and connect with other professionals. If your business targets other businesses or professionals, LinkedIn is an essential platform.

TikTok: TikTok is a newer platform that has quickly gained popularity, especially among younger audiences. It's focused on short, creative videos that often go viral. TikTok is ideal for businesses that want to showcase their creativity and connect with a younger demographic in a fun, entertaining way.

Pinterest: Pinterest is a platform that allows users to discover and save ideas for various interests, from fashion to home decor. It's highly visual and works well for businesses that offer products or services that can be showcased through images, such as retail, food, or design.

5.3 Creating Engaging Content

Creating engaging content is key to success on social media. Your content should resonate with your audience, encourage interaction, and reflect your brand's personality. Here are some tips to help you create content that stands out:

Know Your Audience: Understanding your audience is crucial to creating content that they'll love. What are their interests? What challenges do they face? What kind of content do they enjoy? Use this information to create content that speaks directly to them.

Be Consistent: Consistency is important when it comes to social media. This doesn't just mean posting regularly, but also maintaining a consistent voice, style, and message. Whether you're sharing a blog post, a photo, or a video, your content should always reflect your brand's identity.

Use Visuals: Visual content, such as images and videos, is more likely to catch attention and engage your audience. Make sure your visuals are high-quality, relevant, and aligned with your brand's aesthetic. Use tools like Canva or Adobe Spark to create professional-looking graphics even if you're not a designer.

Tell a Story: Storytelling is a powerful way to connect with your audience. Share stories about your brand, your customers, or your industry. For example, you might post about how your business started, highlight a customer success story, or share the journey behind creating a new product.

Encourage Interaction: Social media is all about interaction, so encourage your audience to engage with your content. Ask questions, run polls, host contests, and respond to comments. The more your audience interacts with your content, the more visible it becomes.

Leverage User-Generated Content: User-generated content (UGC) is content created by your customers or followers that features your brand. This could be a photo of them using your product, a review, or a mention in a post. Sharing UGC not only provides social proof but also encourages others to engage with your brand.

5.4 Measuring Success

To know if your social media efforts are paying off, it's important to measure your success. This means tracking key metrics that show how your content is performing and how your audience is interacting with your brand.

Engagement: Engagement refers to how people are interacting with your content. This includes likes, comments, shares, and retweets. High engagement usually means that your content is resonating with your audience.

Reach: Reach is the number of people who see your content. The more people your content reaches, the more potential customers you can attract. You can increase your reach by posting consistently, using relevant hashtags, and engaging with your audience.

Follower Growth: The number of followers you have can indicate how your audience is growing over time. While follower count isn't the only measure of success, a steady increase in followers suggests that more people are interested in your brand.

Website Traffic: If you're using social media to drive traffic to your website, track how many visitors are coming from your social media channels. Tools like Google Analytics can help you see which platforms are driving the most traffic and which content is most effective.

Conversions: Conversions are the actions you want your audience to take, such as making a purchase, signing up for a newsletter, or downloading a resource. Tracking conversions helps you understand how well your social media efforts are contributing to your overall business goals.

Customer Feedback: Pay attention to what your audience is saying about your brand on social media. Positive feedback can reinforce your efforts, while negative feedback can highlight areas for improvement. Use this feedback to refine your social media strategy and better meet your audience's needs.

Chapter 6: Email Marketing

6.1 What is Email Marketing?

Email marketing is a powerful way to connect with your audience directly through their inbox. It involves sending promotional messages, updates, and information to people who have opted in to receive emails from you. Unlike social media, where your posts might get lost in a feed, emails go straight to the recipient's inbox, making it a more personal and direct way to communicate.

Why Email Marketing Matters: Email marketing is important because it allows you to maintain a direct line of communication with your audience. It's an effective tool for building relationships, nurturing leads, and driving sales. With email marketing, you can reach people who are already interested in your products or services, which increases the likelihood of engagement and conversion.

For example, if you run an online store, you can use email marketing to send out newsletters featuring new products, special offers, and exclusive discounts. This keeps your customers informed and encourages them to make a purchase.

6.2 Building Your Email List

The success of your email marketing efforts depends on having a strong and engaged email list. Your email list is made up of people who have given you permission to send them emails. Here's how to build and grow your list:

Create Signup Forms: Place email signup forms on your website, blog, and social media profiles to make it easy for people to subscribe. Offer a compelling reason for them to join your list, such as a discount, free resource, or exclusive content.

Offer Incentives: Encourage people to subscribe by offering incentives like discounts, free trials, or downloadable resources. For example, if you run a fitness blog, you could offer a free e-book on workout routines in exchange for an email subscription.

Leverage Existing Customers: If you already have customers, invite them to join your email list by promoting it at checkout, on your website, or through follow-up emails. Make sure they understand the value they'll receive by subscribing.

Host Webinars or Events: Webinars, online workshops, or in-person events can be a great way to collect email addresses. Attendees can sign up to receive updates or follow-up information, helping you build your list.

Segment Your List: As your list grows, consider segmenting it into different groups based on interests, behavior, or demographics. This allows you to send more targeted and relevant emails, which can improve engagement and conversion rates.

6.3 Crafting Effective Emails

Creating effective emails is key to a successful email marketing campaign. Your emails should be engaging, relevant, and valuable to your subscribers. Here are some tips for crafting emails that get results:

Write Compelling Subject Lines: The subject line is the first thing people see when they receive your email, so it needs to grab their attention. Make it clear, concise, and intriguing. Avoid using all caps or excessive punctuation, as this can come across as spammy.

Personalize Your Emails: Personalization goes beyond just using the recipient's name. Tailor your content based on their preferences, past purchases, or behavior. For example, if a subscriber has shown interest in a specific product, send them updates or offers related to that product.

Provide Value: Make sure your emails offer something of value to your subscribers. This could be useful information, exclusive deals, or helpful tips. Avoid sending emails that are purely promotional; instead, focus on providing content that your audience will find useful and relevant.

Include Clear Calls to Action: Every email should have a clear call to action (CTA) that tells recipients what you want them to do next. Whether it's making a purchase, signing up for a webinar, or reading a blog post, your CTA should be prominent and easy to follow.

Design for Mobile: Many people check their emails on mobile devices, so it's important to ensure your emails are mobile-friendly. Use a responsive design that adjusts to different screen sizes, and keep your layout simple and easy to navigate.

Test and Optimize: Continuously test different elements of your emails, such as subject lines, send times, and content. Use A/B testing to compare different versions of your emails and see which performs better. Analyzing the results will help you refine your strategy and improve your email marketing efforts.

6.4 Measuring Email Marketing Success

To determine how well your email marketing campaigns are performing, you need to track and analyze key metrics. These metrics will help you understand what's working and where there's room for improvement:

Open Rate: The open rate measures the percentage of recipients who open your email. A higher open rate indicates that your subject lines are effective and that your subscribers are interested in your content.

Click-Through Rate (CTR): The click-through rate measures the percentage of recipients who click on a link within your email. A high CTR suggests that your content and calls to action are engaging and compelling.

Conversion Rate: The conversion rate tracks the percentage of recipients who take the desired action, such as making a purchase or signing up for an event. This metric helps you assess the effectiveness of your email in driving actual results.

Bounce Rate: The bounce rate measures the percentage of emails that could not be delivered to recipients' inboxes. A high bounce rate could indicate issues with your email list or deliverability problems.

Unsubscribe Rate: The unsubscribe rate tracks the percentage of subscribers who opt out of receiving your emails. While some unsubscribes are normal, a high rate might suggest that your content is not meeting your subscribers' expectations.

Engagement Metrics: Monitor other engagement metrics such as replies, forwards, and social shares. These can provide additional insights into how your audience is interacting with your emails.

List Growth: Track the growth of your email list over time. A steady increase in subscribers indicates that your signup strategies are working and that your audience is finding value in your emails.

Chapter 7: Pay-Per-Click Advertising (PPC)

7.1 What is PPC Advertising?

Pay-Per-Click (PPC) advertising is a method of online marketing where you pay each time someone clicks on your ad. Unlike traditional advertising, where you pay a fixed amount to display your ad, PPC allows you to pay only when your ad gets a click. This can be an effective way to drive targeted traffic to your website and increase your chances of making a sale.

How PPC Works: When you set up a PPC campaign, you create ads that appear on search engines, social media platforms, or other websites. You choose specific keywords or targeting criteria, and your ad is shown to people who are searching for or interested in those terms. You only pay when someone clicks on your ad and visits your website.

For example, if you run a travel agency and you bid on keywords like "affordable vacation packages," your ad might appear when someone searches for those terms. If they click on your ad and visit your website, you pay a fee, but you have the chance to convert that visitor into a customer.

Why PPC Matters: PPC is important because it offers immediate results and precise targeting. You can quickly drive traffic to your site, and with proper targeting, you can reach people who are actively interested in what you offer. PPC also allows you to control your budget and measure your ROI (return on investment) accurately.

7.2 Setting Up a PPC Campaign

Setting up a successful PPC campaign involves several key steps. Here's a step-by-step guide to help you get started:

1. Define Your Goals: Before you start, clearly define what you want to achieve with your PPC campaign. Are you looking to drive traffic to your website, generate leads, or increase sales? Your goals will influence your campaign strategy and setup.

2. Choose Your Platform: Decide where you want your ads to appear. Common platforms include Google Ads, Bing Ads, Facebook Ads, and Instagram Ads. Each platform has its own strengths and targeting options, so choose the one that best aligns with your goals and audience.

3. Research Keywords: For search engine PPC campaigns, keyword research is crucial. Identify the keywords that are relevant to your business and that potential customers are likely to search for. Tools like Google Keyword Planner can help you find and analyze keywords.

4. Create Compelling Ads: Your ad copy should be clear, concise, and compelling. It should include a strong headline, relevant keywords, and a clear call to action (CTA). Make sure your ad highlights the benefits of your product or service and encourages users to click.

5. Set Your Budget: Determine how much you're willing to spend on your PPC campaign. Most platforms allow you to set a daily or monthly budget. Keep in mind that your budget will affect your ad placement and how often your ad is shown.

6. Choose Your Targeting Options: Most PPC platforms offer various targeting options to help you reach your ideal audience. You can target based on demographics, location, interests, behavior, and more. The more precise your targeting, the more effective your campaign will be.

7. Set Up Tracking and Analytics: To measure the success of your campaign, set up tracking and analytics. This will allow you to monitor your ad performance, track conversions, and calculate your ROI. Tools like Google Analytics can help you track important metrics.

8. Launch Your Campaign: Once you've set everything up, launch your campaign and monitor its performance. Be prepared to make adjustments based on the data and feedback you receive.

7.3 Optimizing Your PPC Campaign

To get the most out of your PPC campaign, you need to continuously optimize it. Optimization involves making adjustments to improve performance and achieve better results. Here are some tips for optimizing your PPC campaign:

1. Monitor Performance Regularly: Keep an eye on your campaign's performance metrics, such as click-through rate

(CTR), conversion rate, and cost-per-click (CPC). Regular monitoring helps you identify what's working and what needs improvement.

2. Refine Your Keywords: Review the performance of your keywords and make adjustments as needed. Add new keywords that are performing well, and remove or adjust bids for keywords that aren't delivering results. Use negative keywords to exclude irrelevant searches that are wasting your budget.

3. Test Ad Variations: Create multiple versions of your ads to see which performs best. Test different headlines, descriptions, and calls to action. A/B testing helps you determine what resonates most with your audience and can improve your CTR and conversions.

4. Optimize Landing Pages: Ensure that your landing pages are relevant to your ads and provide a good user experience. A well-designed landing page with a clear CTA can increase conversions and improve your ROI. Make sure your landing page loads quickly and is mobile-friendly.

5. Adjust Bids and Budget: Based on the performance data, adjust your bids and budget to maximize your results. Increase bids for high-performing keywords and reduce bids for underperforming ones. Adjust your budget allocation based on the platforms and campaigns that deliver the best results.

6. Analyze Competitors: Keep an eye on your competitors' PPC strategies. Analyze their ads, keywords, and landing pages to gain insights and identify opportunities for improvement.

Tools like SpyFu or SEMrush can help you research your competitors.

7. Use Ad Extensions: Many PPC platforms offer ad extensions that allow you to add extra information to your ads, such as phone numbers, site links, or additional text. Ad extensions can improve your ad's visibility and click-through rate.

7.4 Measuring PPC Success

To understand how well your PPC campaign is performing, you need to measure key metrics. These metrics will help you gauge the effectiveness of your campaign and make data-driven decisions:

1. Click-Through Rate (CTR): The CTR measures the percentage of people who click on your ad after seeing it. A higher CTR indicates that your ad is relevant and engaging.

2. Cost-Per-Click (CPC): CPC is the amount you pay each time someone clicks on your ad. Monitoring CPC helps you manage your budget and determine the cost-effectiveness of your campaign.

3. Conversion Rate: The conversion rate tracks the percentage of visitors who take a desired action after clicking on your ad. A higher conversion rate indicates that your landing page and CTA are effective.

4. Cost-Per-Conversion (CPC): CPC measures how much it costs to acquire a customer or lead through your PPC campaign.

It helps you understand the return on investment for your advertising spend.

5. Quality Score: Quality Score is a metric used by search engines to measure the relevance and quality of your ads, keywords, and landing pages. A higher Quality Score can improve your ad placement and reduce your CPC.

6. Return on Ad Spend (ROAS): ROAS measures the revenue generated for every dollar spent on advertising. It helps you evaluate the profitability of your PPC campaign.

7. Impressions: Impressions indicate how many times your ad is shown to users. While impressions don't measure engagement directly, they provide insight into your ad's visibility and reach.

Chapter 8: The Future of Digital Marketing

8.1 Emerging Trends in Digital Marketing

As technology continues to evolve, digital marketing is constantly changing. Staying ahead of emerging trends is crucial for maintaining a competitive edge. Here are some key trends shaping the future of digital marketing:

1. Artificial Intelligence (AI) and Machine Learning: AI and machine learning are revolutionizing digital marketing by enabling more personalized and data-driven strategies. AI can analyze vast amounts of data to predict consumer behavior, optimize ad campaigns, and automate content creation. Chatbots powered by AI are also becoming more sophisticated, providing instant customer support and enhancing user experience.

2. Voice Search Optimization: With the rise of smart speakers and voice assistants like Amazon's Alexa and Google Assistant, voice search is becoming more prevalent. Marketers need to optimize their content for voice search by focusing on natural language queries and conversational keywords. This shift emphasizes the importance of answering questions and providing concise, relevant information.

3. Video Marketing: Video continues to be a dominant content format, with platforms like YouTube, TikTok, and Instagram

Reels driving engagement. Live streaming and interactive video content are gaining popularity, allowing brands to connect with their audience in real-time and create immersive experiences. Investing in high-quality video content can enhance your brand's visibility and engagement.

4. Influencer Marketing Evolution: Influencer marketing is evolving beyond traditional partnerships. Micro-influencers, who have smaller but highly engaged audiences, are gaining traction for their authenticity and niche appeal. Brands are also exploring long-term collaborations and co-creating content with influencers to build deeper connections with their audience.

5. Privacy and Data Security: As concerns about data privacy grow, regulations like the General Data Protection Regulation (GDPR) and California Consumer Privacy Act (CCPA) are shaping how businesses handle customer data. Marketers need to prioritize transparency, obtain consent, and ensure compliance with privacy regulations to build trust and avoid legal issues.

6. Augmented Reality (AR) and Virtual Reality (VR): AR and VR technologies are enhancing user experiences by providing immersive and interactive content. Brands are using AR for virtual try-ons, product demonstrations, and interactive ads. VR offers virtual tours and experiences that allow users to engage with products in a virtual environment.

7. Personalization: Personalization is becoming increasingly important in digital marketing. Tailoring content, offers, and recommendations based on individual preferences and behavior can significantly improve user experience and conversion rates.

Leveraging data and AI to create personalized experiences can help build stronger customer relationships.

8. Social Commerce: Social media platforms are integrating e-commerce features, allowing users to shop directly within the app. Instagram Shopping, Facebook Shops, and TikTok's shopping capabilities are making it easier for brands to reach consumers and drive sales through social media.

8.2 Adapting to Changes in Digital Marketing

To thrive in the evolving digital landscape, businesses need to be adaptable and proactive. Here's how to stay ahead:

1. Embrace Innovation: Stay informed about new technologies and trends in digital marketing. Experiment with emerging tools and strategies to keep your marketing efforts fresh and relevant. Being open to innovation can give you a competitive advantage.

2. Invest in Continuous Learning: Digital marketing is a dynamic field with constant changes. Invest in ongoing education and training for yourself and your team. Attend webinars, workshops, and conferences to stay updated on the latest developments and best practices.

3. Focus on Data-Driven Decision Making: Use data and analytics to guide your marketing decisions. Regularly review performance metrics, conduct A/B testing, and analyze customer behavior to make informed choices. Data-driven insights can help you optimize your strategies and achieve better results.

4. Foster Customer Relationships: Building strong relationships with your customers is crucial for long-term success. Engage with your audience through personalized communication, provide exceptional customer service, and gather feedback to improve your offerings. Happy customers are more likely to become loyal advocates for your brand.

5. Adapt to Privacy Regulations: Ensure that your marketing practices comply with data privacy regulations. Implement transparent data collection practices, obtain user consent, and provide options for users to manage their preferences. Protecting customer data and respecting privacy concerns can enhance trust and credibility.

6. Optimize for Mobile: Mobile usage continues to rise, making mobile optimization essential. Ensure that your website and content are mobile-friendly, with responsive design and fast load times. A seamless mobile experience can improve user satisfaction and drive conversions.

7. Monitor Competitors: Keep an eye on your competitors' digital marketing strategies to identify opportunities and threats. Analyze their content, campaigns, and customer interactions to gain insights and refine your own approach.

8.3 Looking Ahead

The future of digital marketing is bright and full of possibilities. As technology continues to advance, new opportunities will arise for brands to connect with their audience in innovative ways. By staying informed, adapting to changes, and focusing on delivering value to your customers, you can navigate the evolving digital landscape and achieve continued success.

In summary, the key to thriving in digital marketing is to embrace change, leverage new technologies, and always put your customers first. As you look ahead, remember that staying ahead of trends and continuously improving your strategies will set you apart from the competition and drive your success in the digital world.

Chapter 9: The Digital Marketing Revolution: A Modern Fairytale

Once upon a time, in a bustling kingdom called Marketville, there was a small bakery named "Sweet Delights." The bakery was known far and wide for its delicious pastries and warm, inviting atmosphere. Despite its popularity among the locals, Sweet Delights struggled to attract customers from neighboring towns.

The bakery's owner, Lily, was passionate about baking and loved her craft. However, she faced a challenge: how could she spread the word about her bakery beyond Marketville? The answer seemed elusive, and Lily felt frustrated as her competitors in neighboring towns started to gain recognition.

One day, while Lily was enjoying a cup of tea, a wise old merchant named Jasper visited her bakery. Jasper was known for his vast knowledge of trade and had traveled across many lands. He noticed Lily's concern and offered her some advice.

"Lily," Jasper said with a kind smile, "your bakery has something special, but you need a way to share your story with the world. Have you considered the power of digital marketing?"

Lily was intrigued but confused. "Digital marketing? What's that?"

Jasper explained, "Digital marketing is like magic in the modern world. It allows you to use the internet to reach people far and wide. Imagine being able to share your delicious pastries with not just the people in Marketville but with everyone in neighboring towns and beyond. You can create a digital presence that tells your story and connects with potential customers."

Excited by the idea, Lily decided to give digital marketing a try. She started by building a website for Sweet Delights. Jasper helped her set up a blog where she shared recipes, baking tips, and the stories behind her favorite pastries. With a little guidance, Lily also created profiles on social media platforms like Facebook and Instagram.

As Lily began to share photos of her mouth-watering pastries and behind-the-scenes glimpses of her bakery, she noticed something incredible. People from neighboring towns started to take notice. They began following Sweet Delights on social media, leaving positive comments, and even sharing Lily's posts with their friends.

One day, a well-known food blogger named Emma came across one of Lily's posts. Emma was captivated by the vibrant photos and the heartwarming story of Sweet Delights. She decided to visit the bakery and wrote a glowing review on her popular blog.

The review went viral, and soon Sweet Delights became the talk of the region. People traveled from distant lands just to taste Lily's pastries. The once-small bakery was now a renowned destination, all thanks to the power of digital marketing.

Lily was overjoyed and grateful for Jasper's advice. Digital marketing had transformed her business, helping her reach new audiences and share her passion for baking with the world. She realized that by embracing digital marketing, she had not only grown her customer base but also connected with people who truly appreciated her craft.

As the story of Sweet Delights spread, other businesses in Marketville took notice. They began to explore digital marketing themselves, discovering how it could help them grow and thrive in the digital age.

And so, in the kingdom of Marketville, the lesson was clear: Digital marketing was not just a tool but a gateway to endless possibilities. It had the power to turn dreams into reality and bring people together in ways never imagined before.

Lily continued to bake her delicious pastries, but now with a broader audience who cherished her creations. And Jasper's wisdom lived on, reminding everyone that embracing the magic of digital marketing could make all the difference in the world.

This modern fairytale highlights the transformative power of digital marketing and how it can help businesses reach new heights by connecting with a wider audience.

FAQ: Digital Marketing

1. What is digital marketing?

Digital marketing is the use of digital channels, platforms, and technologies to promote products or services and connect with target audiences. It includes online strategies such as search engine optimization (SEO), social media marketing, content marketing, email marketing, and digital advertising.

2. Why is digital marketing important?

Digital marketing is important because it allows businesses to reach a wider audience, track their marketing efforts, and engage with customers in real-time. It offers targeted, measurable, and cost-effective ways to promote products and services compared to traditional marketing methods.

3. What are the key components of digital marketing?

The key components of digital marketing include SEO, content marketing, social media marketing, email marketing, pay-per-click (PPC) advertising, and analytics. Each component plays a role in attracting, engaging, and converting potential customers.

4. How does SEO work?

SEO (Search Engine Optimization) involves optimizing a website's content, structure, and technical elements to improve its visibility in search engine results pages (SERPs). It includes keyword research, on-page optimization, backlink building, and technical SEO to enhance a site's ranking and drive organic traffic.

5. What is content marketing?

Content marketing is a strategy that involves creating and distributing valuable, relevant, and consistent content to attract and engage a target audience. It aims to build trust, provide information, and drive customer action through blog posts, videos, infographics, and other content types.

6. What is social media marketing?

Social media marketing involves using social media platforms (like Facebook, Instagram, Twitter, LinkedIn) to promote products, engage with customers, and build brand awareness. It includes creating and sharing content, running ads, and interacting with followers.

7. How can I measure the success of my digital marketing efforts?

You can measure the success of digital marketing efforts using various metrics, such as website traffic, conversion rates, engagement rates, click-through rates (CTR), and return on investment (ROI). Analytics tools like Google Analytics can provide insights into performance.

8. What is pay-per-click (PPC) advertising?

PPC advertising is a model where advertisers pay a fee each time their ad is clicked. It typically involves bidding on keywords and displaying ads on search engine results pages or other platforms. It's a way to drive targeted traffic to a website quickly.

9. How does email marketing work?

Email marketing involves sending promotional messages, updates, or newsletters to a list of subscribers via email. It's used to nurture leads, drive sales, and keep customers informed. Effective email marketing includes segmentation, personalization, and optimizing email content.

10. What is the role of analytics in digital marketing?

Analytics play a crucial role in digital marketing by providing data on campaign performance, user behavior, and website traffic. This information helps marketers make data-driven decisions, optimize strategies, and measure the effectiveness of their efforts.

11. How often should I update my website content?

It's recommended to update your website content regularly to keep it fresh, relevant, and engaging. Regular updates can also improve SEO and user experience. Aim to publish new content or refresh existing content at least once a month.

12. What is influencer marketing?

Influencer marketing involves partnering with individuals who have a large and engaged following on social media or other platforms. Influencers promote products or services to their audience, leveraging their credibility and reach to drive brand awareness and sales.

13. How can I improve my website's SEO?

To improve your website's SEO, focus on keyword research, optimize on-page elements (like titles, meta descriptions, and headings), build high-quality backlinks, improve site speed, and ensure your site is mobile-friendly. Regularly updating content and addressing technical issues also helps.

14. What is a content calendar, and why is it important?

A content calendar is a schedule that outlines what content will be published and when. It helps organize and plan content creation, ensures consistency, and aligns content with marketing goals and key dates. It also helps avoid gaps and overlaps in content.

15. What are the best practices for social media marketing?

Best practices for social media marketing include creating engaging and relevant content, posting consistently, using visuals, interacting with your audience, leveraging hashtags, monitoring analytics, and staying updated with trends. Tailor content to each platform for maximum impact.

16. How can I use data to drive my digital marketing strategy?

Use data to drive your digital marketing strategy by analyzing performance metrics, identifying trends, and understanding customer behavior. Data helps you make informed decisions, optimize campaigns, and allocate resources effectively to achieve your marketing goals.

17. What are the benefits of using video in marketing?

Video marketing offers numerous benefits, including increased engagement, higher retention rates, better storytelling, and improved SEO. Videos can showcase products, demonstrate features, and connect with audiences on a personal level, making them a powerful marketing tool.

18. What is mobile marketing?

Mobile marketing involves reaching and engaging with customers through mobile devices such as smartphones and tablets. It includes strategies like mobile-friendly websites, SMS marketing, app-based marketing, and location-based promotions.

19. How can I build a strong online presence for my business?

To build a strong online presence, focus on creating valuable content, optimizing your website for search engines, engaging with your audience on social media, and leveraging digital advertising. Consistency, quality, and authenticity are key to establishing a compelling online presence.

20. What are some common mistakes in digital marketing to avoid?

Common mistakes in digital marketing to avoid include neglecting SEO, failing to define clear goals, ignoring data and analytics, not targeting the right audience, and being inconsistent with content and messaging. Avoiding these mistakes can help improve the effectiveness of your marketing efforts.

References of Successful People Who Achieved Success Through Digital Marketing

1. **Gary Vaynerchuk**
   Gary Vaynerchuk, entrepreneur and CEO of VaynerMedia, started by taking his family's wine business online through the use of social media and digital content. His strategic use of platforms like YouTube and Twitter transformed a small liquor store into a multi-million-dollar enterprise. Today, he is a highly sought-after digital marketing expert and author.

2. **Neil Patel**
   Neil Patel is a digital marketing guru known for his SEO expertise. Co-founder of successful businesses like Crazy Egg, Hello Bar, and KISSmetrics, Neil leveraged content marketing and SEO to build a personal brand that made him one of the most influential figures in digital marketing. His website and blog are go-to resources for marketers worldwide.

3. **Sophia Amoruso**
   Founder of Nasty Gal and author of the bestselling book *#GIRLBOSS*, Sophia Amoruso built her fashion empire primarily through digital marketing. By utilizing platforms like MySpace and Instagram to connect with her audience, she was able to grow a small eBay store into a massive e-commerce business.

4. **Rand Fishkin**

Rand Fishkin, founder of Moz, used digital marketing to become a thought leader in the SEO space. By creating insightful content, including blog posts and webinars, he transformed Moz from a small SEO consulting company into a leading software provider and educational resource for marketers.

5. **PewDiePie (Felix Kjellberg)**
PewDiePie, the popular YouTube content creator, leveraged the power of digital marketing and social media to become one of the most subscribed individual YouTubers. His gaming videos and engaging content attracted millions of viewers and allowed him to build a massive online presence.

6. **Pat Flynn**
Pat Flynn is the founder of Smart Passive Income and became a successful digital entrepreneur by creating valuable online content. He focused on podcasts, blogging, and affiliate marketing to build a thriving community and income stream, inspiring others to follow the same digital marketing strategies for passive income.

7. **Michelle Phan**
Michelle Phan is a beauty influencer who gained fame through her YouTube makeup tutorials. Through her use of digital platforms, she built a personal brand and launched her own makeup line, EM Cosmetics. Her success demonstrates the power of content creation and influencer marketing.

8. **Joe Pulizzi**
Joe Pulizzi, founder of the Content Marketing

Institute, grew his career by mastering content marketing. He built a community around teaching content marketing strategies, publishing blogs, and hosting events like Content Marketing World, which became the world's largest content marketing event.

9. **Tim Ferriss**
   Best known for his book *The 4-Hour Workweek*, Tim Ferriss used digital marketing to turn his personal brand into a success story. By utilizing podcasting, blogging, and email marketing, Ferriss grew a loyal audience and built a media empire that includes books, courses, and speaking engagements.

10. **Andrew Chen**
    Andrew Chen is a growth hacking expert who used digital marketing strategies to help companies like Uber scale rapidly. His focus on user acquisition and data-driven marketing campaigns allowed him to help several startups grow into successful businesses.

These examples highlight how digital marketing played a crucial role in propelling these individuals to success across various industries, from e-commerce to personal branding and tech startups.

Conclusion

Digital marketing has transformed the way businesses connect with their audiences. The rise of the internet, social media, and mobile technology has revolutionized marketing strategies, creating a world where traditional methods are no longer sufficient to stay competitive. From SEO to content marketing, social media engagement, and data-driven decision-making, digital marketing offers unparalleled opportunities for businesses to expand their reach, build brand loyalty, and drive sales.

Throughout this book, we've explored the essential components of digital marketing. We've discussed the importance of establishing a strong online presence, the power of content to engage audiences, and the strategic use of SEO and PPC to boost visibility and drive traffic. We've examined the influence of social media on consumer behavior and how email marketing and automation can nurture leads and maintain customer relationships. Through each chapter, we've seen how these elements come together to create a comprehensive digital marketing strategy that can help businesses thrive in today's digital landscape.

One of the key takeaways from this guide is that digital marketing is not a one-size-fits-all solution. Every business is unique, with different goals, audiences, and challenges. Digital marketing allows for customization and flexibility, enabling businesses to tailor their strategies to meet their specific needs. Whether you're a small business owner looking to expand your local reach or a large corporation aiming to grow your global footprint, digital marketing provides the tools to do so efficiently and effectively.

Moreover, digital marketing is continuously evolving. New technologies, platforms, and consumer trends are constantly shaping the landscape, which means that marketers must stay informed and adaptable. The principles of digital marketing outlined in this book serve as a foundation, but staying current with emerging trends and continually refining strategies is essential for long-term success.

In addition to the tactical aspects, the heart of digital marketing is understanding your audience. The ability to connect with customers on a personal level, engage them through meaningful content, and respond to their needs is what sets great marketers apart. In the digital world, personalization, authenticity, and transparency are more important than ever. Consumers are savvy; they can spot inauthentic messages a mile away, and they gravitate toward brands that show genuine interest in solving their problems and adding value to their lives.

Another critical point is the importance of data. Digital marketing offers something that traditional marketing often couldn't—measurability. Analytics, metrics, and data insights allow marketers to understand what works and what doesn't, providing the opportunity to optimize campaigns and improve ROI. As we've discussed, using data effectively can help refine strategies, target the right audiences, and enhance customer experiences. But beyond just collecting data, knowing how to interpret and apply it is key to driving successful marketing outcomes.

Looking ahead, the future of digital marketing will continue to be shaped by innovation. Artificial intelligence, machine learning, augmented reality, voice search, and other emerging technologies are beginning to play more significant roles in marketing strategies. As these technologies develop, they will open new doors for marketers to engage with consumers in more personalized and immersive ways. The businesses that embrace these advancements and incorporate them into their digital marketing strategies will likely be the ones that thrive.

The story of digital marketing is also a story of empowerment. It has leveled the playing field for businesses of all sizes. Small businesses that may not have the resources for large-scale traditional advertising can now compete with bigger players through smart, targeted digital strategies. Entrepreneurs can build personal brands and connect with global audiences with little more than a laptop and an internet connection. Companies can create meaningful, long-lasting relationships with their customers by meeting them where they are—online, across various platforms and devices.

In essence, digital marketing is about more than just selling products or services; it's about building relationships and creating value for your audience. It's about understanding the needs and desires of your customers and delivering solutions that resonate with them on a deeper level. By focusing on the customer experience and constantly seeking to improve and innovate, businesses can not only survive but thrive in the competitive digital world.

As you move forward in your digital marketing journey, remember that success doesn't happen overnight. It takes time, effort, experimentation, and learning. Mistakes will be made along the way, but each misstep offers a chance to learn and improve. Stay curious, stay flexible, and keep pushing forward. The digital marketing landscape is vast and full of possibilities. With the right strategies, tools, and mindset, you can harness its power to achieve your business goals.

In conclusion, *The Essential Guide to Digital Marketing* is just the beginning. The real work comes from applying these insights to your unique situation and continuously adapting to the ever-changing digital environment. Whether you're looking to increase brand awareness, drive more traffic, boost conversions, or build lasting customer relationships, digital marketing has the potential to unlock growth and innovation. Embrace the challenges, stay committed to learning, and watch as your business evolves and thrives in the digital age.

Don't miss out!

Visit the website below and you can sign up to receive emails whenever Naveen Sharma publishes a new book. There's no charge and no obligation.

https://books2read.com/r/B-A-EYYEC-DJYOE

BOOKS2READ

Connecting independent readers to independent writers.

www.ingramcontent.com/pod-product-compliance
Lightning Source LLC
Chambersburg PA
CBHW030050230526
45471CB00003B/1022